Bitcoin Cash versus Bitcoin
The battle of the cryptocurrencies

By Johan von Amsterdam

INTRODUCTION

In recent times, the world of cryptocurrency has been gripped by the ever growing rift with regard to how Bitcoin (BTC), the most successful cryptocurrency in history can be improved. The Kafkaesque nature of the controversy resulted in a hard fork on the 1st of August 2017, which, in turn, brought about a split in Bitcoin (BTC) to what is now known as Bitcoin Cash (referred to as BCH or BCC[1]) and BTC (the original Bitcoin) itself. But what is the difference between these two currencies and what does this mean for new investors who are willing to stake their money on both Bitcoins, and what are the short and long term implications of these events for the average holders of these currencies?

---

1) *The most common abbreviation for Bitcoin cash is BCH, but sometimes also BCC is used to refer to Bitcoin cash.*
In this book only BCH will be used further on when referencing to Bitcoin cash.

Profoundly, this book not only seeks to address a lot of these issues but serves as an essential guide for beginners in cryptocurrencies, especially Bitcoin. Amazingly, it simply walks the reader through the history and features of cryptocurrencies, the underlying principles behind their operation, what makes Bitcoin tick, among several other important issues. With Bitcoin increasingly gaining traction in usage all over the world, it is pertinent to note that people are less likely to invest their money in any venture they know virtually nothing about; as a result, this book is designed to make critical information as simple as possible for new and existing investors.

Furthermore, it is meant to serve as a quick guide to Bitcoin Cash, were to buy and store it.

A gift as a thank you!

The cryptocurrency world is a fast moving world. Knowledge is power and the world of the cryptocurrencies keeps evolving.

If you want to stay up-to-date, please check out the author's website:

www.aboutcryptocurrencies.net.

Here you will find the latest cryptocurrencies news gathered from around the world and updated multiple times per day. Sign-up for the 'Daily Crypto News' and receive the electronic version of the officially published book: 'Bitcoin: What is Bitcoin?' for free as a thank you for buying this book.

So go to www.aboutcryptocurrencies.net, sign up and get the **ebook for free** as a thank you.

Enough, let's get started.

© Copyright - All rights reserved.

This document is geared towards providing exact and reliable information in regards to the topic and issue covered. The publication is sold with the idea that the publisher is not required to render accounting, officially permitted, or otherwise, qualified services. If advice is necessary, legal or professional, a practiced individual in the profession should be ordered.

- From a Declaration of Principles which was accepted and approved equally by a Committee of the American Bar Association and a Committee of Publishers and Associations.

In no way is it legal to reproduce, duplicate, or transmit any part of this document in either electronic means or in printed format. Recording of this publication is strictly prohibited and any storage of this document is not allowed unless with written permission from the publisher. All rights reserved.

The information provided herein is stated to be truthful and consistent, in that any liability, in terms of inattention or otherwise, by any usage or abuse of any policies, processes, or directions contained within is the solitary and utter responsibility of the recipient reader. Under no circumstances will any legal responsibility or blame be held against the publisher for any reparation, damages, or monetary loss due to the information herein, either directly or indirectly.

Respective authors own all copyrights not held by the publisher.

The information herein is offered for informational purposes solely, and is universal as so. The presentation of the information is without contract or any type of guarantee assurance.

The trademarks that are used are without any consent, and the publication of the trademark is without permission or backing by the trademark owner. All trademarks and brands within this book are for clarifying purposes only and are the owned by the owners themselves, not affiliated with this document.

TABLE OF CONTENTS

1: INTRODUCTION TO CRYPTOCURRENCIES	5
2: THE BASICS OF BITCOIN	8
3: BITCOIN PROTOCOLS	12
4: BITCOIN PRIVATE KEYS	18
5: BETWEEN A HARD AND A SOFT FORK!	21
6: BTC VERSUS BCH	26
5: THE SPLIT!	29
7: AFTERMATH OF THE BITCOIN SPLIT	33
Thank you!	35

1: INTRODUCTION TO CRYPTOCURRENCIES

WHAT IS CRYPTOCURRENCY

A cryptocurrency can be defined as a part of alternative currencies, virtual cash or digital asset that is intended for use as a medium of exchange while employing the use of cryptography as a technique to secure transactions and to take the creation of other units of the currency under management and control. For the sake of clarity, cryptography is the study of methods of creating and evaluating protocols that put a stop to third parties from reading concealed messages.

THE HISTORY OF CRYPTOCURRENCIES

The forerunners of today's cryptocurrencies are the "b-money," which was a proposal and concept in the late 90s on a digital monetary system published by Wei Dai, a computer Engineer, and the "Bit Gold," a precursor of Bitcoin that was created by Nick Szabo. In fact, Wei Dai's work and ideas were much identical to the Bitcoin scheme in use today, but he insisted that the concepts were developed independently of one another.

In 2009, a mysterious developer that goes by the pseudonym Satoshi Nakamoto created the first decentralized cryptocurrency, which is the bitcoin. Consequently, other cryptocurrencies such as Litecoin, Peercoinwas, Namecoin, Zcash, Dash, Ethereum, Rippx among several others have since come on board. Each of them has a broad range of features that seek to address specific issues plaguing the world of cryptocurrency.

FEATURES

- Owing to the technology and security attributes they possess, it is hard to make counterfeits of cryptocurrencies.
- Another essential characteristic of cryptocurrencies that might make them more appealing is the fact that they are organic; in essence it means that they are not created by a government or Central authority.
- What being decentralized means in effect is that they are, in theory, free from any form of meddling or manipulation.
- Unlike centralized currencies, nearly all crypto currencies are supposed to reduce in production in due course. For

instance, Bitcoin is never going to exceed a market cap of 21 million coins that will be in circulation over time.

- Although a variety of cryptocurrency specifications are obtainable today, nearly all of them are the result of any of two protocols referred to as proof –of-work or proof-of stake.
- Every cryptocurrency often relies on a community of miners that help validate and process transactions with the use of their ASIC machines. Without a doubt, the contributions of miners are immense and invaluable in the sustenance of the entire system.
- Due to the cryptographic technology behind it, the users of crypto currencies are afforded some degree of anonymity making it hard for law enforcement agencies to seize them, unlike centralized currencies.

THE PROS AND CONS OF CRYPTOCURRENCIES

- Cryptocurrencies ensure the secure transfer of funds is carried out with ease.
- When compared with the amount charged by traditional financial institutions for the transfer of funds, the transmission of funds via cryptocurrencies comes at negligible processing fees, which makes it even more appealing to users.

- The technology behind the Bitcoin's blockchain which is a sort of online ledger that helps maintain every transaction that's ever been carried out by means of Bitcoins is being explored by experts for its potentials in crowdfunding, online voting and efficient processing of payments that could bring about a reduction of transaction fees in the Banking industry.
- Due to the inherent nature of cryptocurrencies as virtual or digital money which is lacking a centralized repository, their balances are more susceptible to complete obliteration during a system crash, especially if no backup is maintained. Furthermore, their online ledgers may be prone to attacks from hackers.
- The market prices of crypto currencies are dependent on sentiments that fuels supply and demand, thereby making the rate at which they are exchanged move backward and forward widely.

2: THE BASICS OF BITCOIN

As stated earlier, Bitcoin is a digital currency that was created in 2009 by Satoshi Nakamoto who mined the first Bitcoin circulation. Bitcoin is one of the pioneering cryptocurrencies that employ the use of a peer-to-peer payment technology to aid in facilitating immediate payments or transactions. Being a virtual currency like all crypto currencies, Bitcoin is not owned by banks, stock exchanges, organization, governments, and company.

THE WORKINGS OF BITCOIN

BITCOIN ESSENTIALS

- For new users to get familiarized with the use of Bitcoin, they must first obtain a Bitcoin wallet software that will help encrypt and maintain Bitcoin balances on either their computer or mobile phone devices.
- Since most wallet software is downloadable, all you have to do is to download and install it on your devices.
- As soon as you have installed wallet software on any device of your choice, you may generate a Bitcoin address and share them with people to make payment to you or for you to pay to them. Also, you can generate as

many Bitcoin addresses as your need for them warrants, but a Bitcoin address must only be utilized on one occasion for your anonymity to be sustained.

- Afterward, the investor can purchase Bitcoins via other payment means like credit card or bank account and fill up their wallet with the Bitcoins
- The adoption of Bitcoin as a medium of exchange is fast gaining popularity as it can be employed to settle transactions at dentists, groceries, clothing stores, online retailers, vehicle purchases, restaurants, and even for property rentals.
- Aside from using it to make payments for purchases, you can also make a fortune from speculating in Bitcoin itself. Such speculation centers on staking Bitcoins in the hope that it will go up in value.
- The least unit of Bitcoin is the Satoshi and is gotten when Bitcoin is dividable into eight decimal places, which is100 millionth of one Bitcoin. If the miners taking part agree to the change, Bitcoin could still be further split into more decimal places.

UNDERSTANDING THE BLOCKCHAIN

A blockchain is the shared public ledger upon which the whole Bitcoin network is dependent and is a record of all transactions that's ever been carried out. The blockchain is regularly on the increase and being updated with fresh records of "blocks" that are deemed to have been 'completed.' To understand this above explanation clearly, you may consider it as a way of assessing the spendable balance of Bitcoin wallets and to verify new transactions to be Bitcoins that can be spent and are really owned by the individual spending them.

FEATURES OF THE BLOCKCHAIN

- The introduction of blocks to the blockchain is done in a linear, chronological order.
- Cryptography is used to ensure the security, integrity and chronological order of the blockchain system.
- Every computer (node) that is linked to the Bitcoin network with the intention of carrying out the validation and conveyance of transactions can automatically access a downloadable copy of the blockchain upon being linked with the Bitcoin network.

- It maintains full information concerning the addresses and their balances right from the origin of the block to the recently completed block.

HOW DOES BLOCKCHAIN WORK?

The block itself is a 'current' aspect of a blockchain that accounts for some or all of the latest transactions, and as soon as it is complete, it moves straight to the blockchain as a long-lasting part of the database. The blockchain is an evidence of each one of such transaction on the Bitcoin network and can be viewed as a significant technological advancement of Bitcoin.

Every time a block becomes complete, a new one is created, and the blockchain has a limitless number of similar blocks in its system. You might want to think that the blocks are not well arranged or arbitrarily positioned in a blockchain, but, in reality, they are connected in an appropriate linear, chronological order, much in the same way chains are linked to one another, with each block holding a hash of the preceding block.

When drawing the comparison of the Bitcoin blockchain system with the traditional banking methods, blockchain can be likened to an entire record of a banking transaction. Another area of similarity is that transactions are chronologically inputted in a blockchain much in the same way bank transactions are entered. Furthermore, blocks can be likened to bank statements.

Every computer or node that takes part in the operation of the system can have access to the blockchain database and is dependent on the Bitcoin protocol in use. The complete copy of the blockchain contains detailed account and history of all Bitcoin transactions ever performed.

It can thus provide insight as regards detailed information on a specific Bitcoin address; such as how much worth or value can be attributed to it at any point in its history. The growing popularity of Bitcoin as a cryptocurrency has resulted in an enormous increase in transactions, and it is estimated that a new block is added to the block chain via mining at an average about 10 minutes apiece. It is important to note that the ever-rising size of the blockchain is regarded by some stakeholders as problems that arose out of storage and harmonization.

WHAT ARE BITCOIN BLOCKS?

Blocks can be defined as files in which data relating to the Bitcoin network is entered or recorded in a lasting manner. The block is designed in such a way that it takes account of several or every one of the most recent Bitcoin transactions that haven't been captured in any past blocks.

As a result, the block functions in the same way as a page of a bank ledger or record book. As soon as a block is deemed to be 'completed,' it gives up to the subsequent block in the blockchain. Another key feature of a block is that it maintains a lasting store of records, which as soon as it is written, can't be changed or gotten rid of.

In summary, since the Bitcoin network is subject to a significant amount of transactional activities, it becomes pertinent to keep an evidence of these transactions so that users can follow the trail of what's been paid, to whom and by whom. The block directly takes a record of transactions that's been carried out within a particular period.

3: BITCOIN PROTOCOLS

The inherent and underlying issues that are often associated with the traditional cryptocurrency made Bitcoin to come up with the use of the blockchain protocol to manage the entire system because Bitcoin is one of the first peer-to-peer payment networks that also works based on a cryptographic protocol. In reality, no particular individual can lay claim to ownership of the bitcoin protocol, but we shall examine the workings of the protocol and also take a look at the major Bitcoin protocols.

HOW DOES BITCOIN PROTOCOL WORK?

Owners of Bitcoins can send and receive coins by just broadcasting digitally signed messages to the network via their bitcoin wallet's software. Since the existing Bitcoin transaction system is reliant on trust, users can only hope that each transaction will bring about a specific outcome. However, the issue is that these electronic payment systems are not to be relied on infrequently, thereby resulting in apprehension about fraud between buyers and sellers.

The problem of deceit or unreliability might be the result of a variety of factors that range from users trying to double-spend their coins or a user making an effort to refuse service from another user or a user looking for ways to exploit the system for financial gains. As a way of putting a check on the issues as mentioned earlier and other possible attacks that may arise; Bitcoin developers set up a system that is dependent on cryptographic proof via the utilization of digital signatures and a very complicated verification process.

USING DIGITAL SIGNATURES FOR VERIFICATION

Blockchain employs the use of a series of digital signatures known as "coin," that is received as soon as a holder passes it on to the next owner. Every time it is transferred, the owner inserts a hash that indicates the past transactions and the public key of the new holder. As the electronic coin goes from one owner to another, notations are all included at the end of it, so as to give a way to verify ownership.

EXTRA LAYER OF TRUST USING TIMESTAMP SERVER AND PROOF-OF-WORK SYSTEM

As a way of ensuring that the same value of coins are not spent more than once or "double spent," Bitcoin developers set up a verification process that determines how the coin is being used. The process employs the use of a timestamp server that inserts a period in time to the hash to confirm or verify the transaction. In addition to that, the timestamp is integrated, together with each change in possession of the coin. Furthermore, a proof-of-work system applies a specific value to the electronic coin to further authenticate every transaction that is carried out with the cryptocurrency.

THE BLOCKCHAIN NETWORK

As mentioned earlier, Bitcoin as a cryptocurrency is decentralized in the sense that it employs a network format whereby fresh transactions are stored into blocks. Afterward, the value or a proof-of-work is added to the block and then relayed throughout the network. Acceptance of the blocks of digital coins is only possible after they have been confirmed valid and verified as being unspent.

New blocks will continue to go through the process of sustaining the movement of the digital coins from one owner to another and being tracked whether it has been spent on specific goods or services with the blockchain network which is also regarded as a kind of ledger. As soon as sufficient blocks are generated from the digital coins, they can then be gotten rid of, to make more disk space available to hold newer blocks.

LINKING CHAINS

MAINTAINING AN HONEST LEDGER

Due to the common threat of fraud that the conventional transaction system was well-known for, it becomes essential for blockchain to try to find a way to make sure that those dealing with these blocks are as sincere as possible. What it means, in essence, is that, for those to whom the task of verifying and recording transactions (miners) on the block to remain honest and sincere, they are to be compensated by way of their digital coins as recompense for honest work.

This way, miners become conscious of the fact that, adhering to the regulations of blockchain a great deal is beneficial than to try and con the system. Miners are individuals or organizations with machines that verify a transaction and include it to the public blockchain so that other miners can have the right to use and bring up to date their own version of the blockchain. For their role and the work they carry out on the blockchain network, miners get rewarded with a little portion of each transaction they execute.

On the other hand, there are a number of backup procedures, which are often in operation on the network or business-owned machines that Bitcoin developers have adopted and enforced to thwart any attack or to prevent bad blocks from the network. A typical case in point of a backup course of action is network alerts which may have been fashioned to go off, once miners discover these bad blocks. Afterward, the alerts and doubtful blocks are pulled and evaluated for any contradictions and then taken out if they are discovered to be invalid.

HOW BLOCKCHAIN FOSTERS PRIVACY AND ANONYMITY

Bitcoin is able to guarantee the privacy of users because the blockchain technology only gives an idea that an individual is sending something to someone else without giving a clue about what is being sent and whether it has to do with currency, information, or any other form of valuable asset. The elimination of a dependable third party and counter party attaches a degree of privacy to the use of electronic cash for transactions. In this fashion, the process of employing the use of cryptocurrency such as Bitcoin gives the holder some degree of anonymity.

MAJOR BITCOIN PROTOCOLS

The growth of Bitcoin as a cryptocurrency since its origin in 2009 has been on a meteoric rise both in size and scope with its notional value reaching in excess of $10 billion and so has its network grown at an exponential rate as well. All through this development, the system started to go through various pains linked to such growth, and they are widely related to scaling up, in order to create room for the huge number and rate of transactions, while maintaining the security, intrinsic worth of privacy, and reduced transaction costs all at once.

At this stage, it is crucial to bear in mind that the novel protocol that was written by Bitcoin's founder, the mysterious Satoshi Nakamoto has turned out to be known as Bitcoin core or Bitcoin QT. And it has led to three rival versions of the Bitcoin protocol; which are the BitPay Core, Bitcoin Classic and Bitcoin Unlimited. The three attempts came in the wake of a contentious roll out of Bitcoin XT that might have resulted in an increase of the block size to 8MB but were mostly rejected by the bitcoin community.

BITPAY CORE

Although BitPay Core is in a trial phase for now, however, its fundamental concept revolves around having two limits. Number one is a 'hard limit' on block size that would be altered on a frequent basis, coinciding with intricate adjustments, and a second 'soft limit' which the miner community will want to make compulsory among themselves and is comparable to the focal points of Bitcoin Unlimited.

BITCOIN CLASSIC

This Bitcoin protocol aims to take the edge off the issues of huge transactions that are leading to transaction log jams and rising transaction costs. The protocol hoped to achieve this by way of increasing the block size, which is the quantity of kilobyte in a block of transactions from 1MB to 2MB. The choice of 2MB was selected on purpose and was dependent on the results of data gathered by its developers, and from interactions with several Bitcoin miners and mining pools. Aside from the support, it has from big mining pools like AntPooland BW Pool, and wallet/exchanges such as Coinbase and OKCoin, the creators of Bitcoin classic states that they have the backing of Gavin Andresen, the past Bitcoin Core lead and Bitcoin XT developer.

BITCOIN UNLIMITED

This Bitcoin protocol as the name implies embraces the nonexistence of a hard-coded block-size limit. As a substitute, it lets users set limits on their nodes manually; the developers look ahead to a compromise on a limit to materialize naturally at an ostensibly Schelling or focal point. The protocol is designed to be a solution that people will be inclined to exploit in the absence of communication since it appears natural, unique, or valuable to them. In addition, it aims to bring in some degree of democracy by letting the community to vote on necessary changes regarding how to develop, manage and implement the protocol.

4: BITCOIN PRIVATE KEYS

A Bitcoin private key can be described as a secret number created to let people spend their Bitcoins or make irreversible transactions. Users are given a Bitcoin private key when they are issued with a Bitcoin address. Typically, it has a 256-bit number and may be used to sell, accept, donate Bitcoin, hence must be kept really safe. For instance, a Bitcoin private key may look like this: *18Qs4IuA5d5ViEiPWYau6fhRTHEFZ9XaLo*.

KEEPING YOUR PRIVATE KEYS SAFE

In the past, several secret/private keys or backup seed have been lost due to the storage medium on which they are saved. Frequently used mediums of storing private keys are listed below with some of their weaknesses.

STORAGE ON A PIECE OF PAPER

Whether the information is written, printed or laminated, a number of things could go wrong with the storage medium, and they are not limited to the following:

- The paper may be discovered and stolen
- The paper could be torn, burnt, spoiled, or damaged by smoke

- A hand-written paper might not be legible; laminated paper is susceptible to being ruined while attempts to print on paper could be unsuccessful if the paper is wet.

STORAGE ON A FLASH DRIVE

- The possibility of breakage exists
- It can be affected by fast changing magnetic fields, for example, MRIs
- They may be affected by fire and smoke
- Many of these drives are not designed for storing things in the long run
- Can become corroded from salt water or some atmospheric conditions
- You may find it hard to retrieve your data from it
- It can be adversely affected by harsh environmental factors
- In general, flash drives aren't recommended for long-term storage

STORAGE IN THE CLOUD

- There is a risk of hackers attempting to steal the private keys
- Other people may have access to your cloud storage and take the keys

STORAGE ON A COMPUTER

- They are susceptible to crashes which make data recovery costly
- Computers are prone to physical attacks and may get burnt or damaged by smoke
- The data on conventional hard disc drive may be degraded by strong magnetic fields and could get destroyed physically.
- Mishaps might occur that will bring about data loss
- It is ill-advised to store up data meant to last for long on Solid state drives (SSDs) if they are not going to be powered.
- If the computer is linked to the internet, it is prone to attacks from hackers who might want to break into it, to steal the key irrespective of the encryption technology employed.
- The use of a computer for storage of private keys is often associated with a broad range of threats like firmware exploits, the use of malicious USB cords and 0-day exploits.
- The use external hard disk drives for storage are limited to just couple of years as a minimum if stored appropriately

- If computer is not linked to the net, the safety it provides is function of the encryption technology used and doesn't negate the fact that an individual may still enter the location illegally and copy the data with no one taking notice

STORAGE ON DIGITAL MEDIA LIKE CD, FLOPPY DISK, LASERDISC, OR MINI-DISC

- There is a high tendency for plastics to stop working after a while.
- Exposure to adverse environmental conditions such as heat, humidity, regular light, all kind of chemicals, and the oxygen in the air may degrade them. It could also result in data loss when private keys are stored on a medium derived from plastic or written/printed on plastic.
- Plastics could get burnt or become damaged by smoke
- The risk of bodily harm occurring exist, thereby making it not viable or costly to recover the lost data
- There is a probability that magnetic media such as tapes and floppy disc could be damaged by magnetic fields

5: BETWEEN A HARD AND A SOFT FORK!

Since Bitcoin operates, based on open source software, which implies that the code is free and accessible for everyone to view and make use of. On the other hand, for individuals or organizations hoping to take part in the Bitcoin network whether as miners, node operators, or wallet administrators; the update and maintenance of the existing versions of the Bitcoin software code vary from essential to very necessary.

With the evolution of Bitcoin as a cryptocurrency, it becomes imperative that several adjustments have to be made to the protocol. These alterations may range from including new feature sets like allowing multi-sig, to altering a core metric of the protocol, such as raising the peak block size.

THE ELEPHANT IN THE ROOM

The core issue is with the speed of the technology which is really slow. Bitcoin network processes around seven transactions in 10 minutes compared to VISA that handles 150 million transactions every day. VISA deals with 1700 transactions per second, and its system has the ability to handle 24000 each second. Users of Bitcoin are increasing every day, and there's no alteration to the core technology that handles their transactions, thereby resulting in network logjams and extensive waiting period for transactions to go through.

THE RUDIMENTS OF FORKS

It is important to note that before now, Bitcoin forks takes place somewhat on a regular basis. A fork is the side-effect of distributed consensus that occurs whenever two miners locate a block almost at the same time. To put it simply, a fork in software development alludes to an event that results in an independent project spinning off from a software project.

The resolution of the uncertainty around such events becomes apparent when successive blocks are added to one, thereby causing it to become the lengthiest chain, whereas the other block becomes "orphaned" or neglected by the network.

However, forks could as well be deliberately set up in the network, and often comes about when developers try to make amends to the rules that the software utilizes to make a decision on whether a transaction is valid or not. For instance, Litecoin, a crypto currency is a fork of Bitcoin since the creators of Litecoin copied Bitcoin's code, carried out some alterations, and then launched a separate project.

As soon as a block is found to have transactions that are invalid, then it is disregarded by the network, and the miner who discovers that block will miss out on a block recompense.

Consequently, miners, in general, would like to mine only blocks that are valid and built on the longest chain. It is vital to keep in mind that changes induced to a protocol often call for either a soft or hard fork of the Bitcoin software. Performing a fork of the Bitcoin software is different from other open source projects since each user operating a Bitcoin node have to sustain their compatibility with the network.

The implication is that any miner that is making use of a Bitcoin software version that isn't suited to the version all and sundry are using may find themselves mining the wrong Blockchain. Nevertheless, miners may bring different versions of the Bitcoin software into play and mine the same Blockchain if the varying versions are well-matched. Here, compatibility is very vital.

Below are some the more widely known forks and their characteristics:

HARD FORK

A hard fork can be described as a software upgrade that sets up a new rule to the network which isn't well-matched with the older software. It could be merely regarded as an extension of the rules. For example, a new rule that permits block size to be 2MB in place of 1MB would have need of a hard fork. A hard fork is complicated in nature as it is an alteration of the Bitcoin protocol, which isn't backward compatible with older versions of the client.

When a hard fork takes place, Nodes that keep on operating on the old version of the software will find newer transactions on the network as being invalid. However, for the entire community to carry on mining valid blocks, every single one of the nodes in the network would have to upgrade to the new rules.

WHAT ARE THE RISKS?

When a hard fork occurs, it could lead to a lot of issues that are not limited to the political fallout that may take place when some sort of political impasse arises, and a fraction of the community prefers to stand by the old rules come what may. In this case, the network computing power or hash rate behind the old chain makes no difference. In fact, what counts the most is the data rule set, since the data is still supposed to have value, which means miners are keen to mine a chain and developers are apt to prop it up. A typical case of how a community might be torn apart over rules is the Ethereum DAO hard fork that resulted in two blockchains employing a variation of the software (Ethereum and Ethereum classic) with both having dissimilar philosophy and currencies.

When a hard fork is performed, the principal risk that may occur is a circumstance whereby nodes on the network using the new software are separated from the earlier version, leading to a fork of the Blockchain. For instance, you may find half of the nodes on the network are using the latest version and mining blocks while the remaining half are mining a different set of blocks by running the older version of the software; which in essence means you will get two dissimilar chains giving rise to a fork of the Blockchain. The scenario given above is quite different from a software fork.

SOFT FORK

On the other hand, a soft fork is any alteration that is backward compatible. For example, a new rule could just let 500 Kilobyte blocks as an alternative to 1MB block. In this situation, nodes that have not been upgraded to be compatible with the new rule will see the new transactions as valid because 500 kilobyte is below 1MB in this scenario. But, should the nodes that haven't been upgraded to be compatible with the new rules keep on mining blocks, the blocks they mine won't be recognized by the nodes that have been updated and rejected as a result. It is for this reason that soft forks require a greater part hash power in the network.

WHAT ARE THE RISKS?

A soft fork that doesn't get a majority of hash power in the network implies that it has very little support and may turn out to be the shortest chain and thus, become orphaned by the network. Otherwise, it may behave in the same vein as a hard fork whereby one chain might just break off. But, if members of the community find it hard to reach a consensus and are separated by such an issue, then the old and new version of Bitcoin might emerge as distinct projects from then on.

It is not all gloom with soft forks because they have mainly been the frequently used choice to upgrade the Bitcoin blockchain nearly all the time, as it is believed that they offer a lesser risk of tearing the network apart. In the past, some soft forks that have gone quite well consists of the P2SH that resulted in the alteration of Bitcoin's address formatting, and the BIP 66 that took care of Bitcoin's signature validation.

USER-ACTIVATED SOFT FORK (UASF)

A user-activated soft fork (UASF) can be described as a contentious proposal that looks at the way a blockchain could add an upgrade, which isn't backed, directly by those stakeholders who makes the network's hashing or computing power available.

The concept of UASF aims to work on the basis that rather than wait for a threshold of support from mining pools, the authority to trigger a soft fork should go to the exchanges, wallets, and companies who are using full nodes. A full node is seen in Bitcoin as one that is still in charge of validating blocks, even though it may not be a mining node.

A greater fraction of key exchanges may have to publicly give their backing to the change, ahead of it being written into a new version of the code. Subsequently, the new software that has been assigned a starting point in the future becomes installed on nodes that would like to partake in the soft fork.

WHAT ARE THE RISKS?

This approach calls for a much longer lead time for it to work than a soft fork that is hash-power-triggered. In fact, it is assumed it could take as much as a year or more to write the code and get all and sundry geared up.

Additionally, if nearly all of the miners end up not agreeing to activate the new rules, they may bring into play their remarkable hash power to divide the network. At present this proposal is hypothetical and hasn't been put into operation.

6: BTC VERSUS BCH

Bitcoin (BTC) is the popular crypto currency that's known all over the world for many years, while in contrast, Bitcoin Cash (BCH) is the projected hard fork that maintained it is closest to Satoshi Nakamoto's original idea for the currency. In order words, BTC and BCH are probable forks of the Bitcoin blockchain.

Before August 1st, 2017 there was a huge debate over the validity of BCH because there was uncertainty whether mining organizations would begin to assign hashing power to it. A move that could end up making it a valid, usable currency with enhanced scalability than the real Bitcoin (BTC) itself, and might even surpass the price of Bitcoin swiftly and turn out to be the default online currency. Otherwise, it might end up being worthless or just like any alt coin out there.

The root of the problem pertains to Bitcoin's legacy code and its capacity of 1MB of data for each block, or around three transactions for every second. The debate had raged for over a year concerning a 'consensus' solution to the problem. Some few days earlier, most key members of, the community had agreed to an upgrade known as Segwit(Segregated Witness) that was locked-in to be wholly put into operation by November 2017.

However, BCH was at variance with the philosophy of Segwit and then made known its plan to increase the block size limit to 8MB by setting off the User Activated Hard Fork (UAHF) on August 1, 2017. Again, supporters of Bitcoin cash considered SegWit to be going against some essential strong points of Bitcoin, such as its decentralization and democratization.

Additionally, they also think SegWit2x was being led by persons with links to shady organizations, and that SegWit2x could be the end of Bitcoin as it is known.

BCH

With its proposal, Bitcoin Cash (BCH) plans to resolve these problems, and it is crucial to bear in mind that one of the most remarkable things about Bitcoin Cash (BCH) is that it gives room for custom block sizing. The increased block size of 8MB proposed by BCH is expected to speed up verification process, and ultimately ensure the survival of the network in spite of the number of miners backing it, albeit with some adjustable degree of difficulty. Its key features include:

- Bitcoin Cash is lead by a client that is referred to as BitcoinABC; where the ABC means "Adjustable Blocksize Cap." In essence, it implies that users may determine their favored blocksize as a result.

- The BCH's default blocksize is set to 2MB, and it has the potential for users to scale it up to 16MB.
- On its official website, BCH defines its currency as being the same as Satoshi's original vision for the coin. It goes on to affirm that *"Bitcoin Cash is peer-to-peer electronic cash for the Internet. It is entirely decentralized, with no central bank and requires no trusted third parties to operate."*

SEGWIT2X

As the August 1st deadline drew nearer, one of two key proposals for enhancing bitcoin's transactional capacity is the SEGWIT2X, which may have gained the most interest. It has the support of a considerable number of prestigious Bitcoin organizations and individuals, the majority of whom are directly associated with the system's startup and investment community. They include nearly all the network's big mining pools, prominent developers such as Gavin Andresen of Bitcoin Core, Bitcoin startups such as Blockchain, BitPay, and Coinbase, among several others.

FEATURES

- SEGWIT was an optimization put forward by Bitcoin Core developer Pieter Wuille in 2015 that aims to increase the number of transactions that go into every block with no

need to raise the block size parameter. In particular, it also takes away the problem of transaction malleability, which may result in a significant improvement of the network if resolved.
- The alterations proposed by SEGWIT2X seek to update the software rules to give room for 2MB blocks. Other rivals with similar objectives to raise Bitcoin's block size parameter such as Bitcoin Unlimited, Bitcoin XT and Bitcoin Classic do not have the same level support as SEGWIT2X.
- Before August 1st, 2017, SEGWIT2X wasn't suggested nor sanctioned by Bitcoin Core, the network's major open-source developer team.
- SEGWIT2X will perform long-anticipated code optimization Segregated Witness (SegWit) that changes the way some data is amassed on the network.
- Its ideas and proposals aren't as fresh but only bring together those proposed earlier by other developers in a new manner.
- As soon as SegWit is activated, it sets a timeline of three months (November 2017), to raise the network's block size from 1MB all the way up to 2MB.

UPDATE

The primary aspect of SegWit2x known as BIP91was locked-in and triggered some days before the scheduled August 1, while BIP148 was to be set off on that day itself. Having locked-in BIP91, a lot of people believed the likelihood of a hard fork was over, but supporters of BCH seem to have other ideas.

5: THE SPLIT!

A TALE OF TWO BITCOINs

On the morning of August 1st, 2017, an attempt to generate another version of the bitcoin blockchain was formally making progress. After overcoming some obstacles that morning, miners managed to create a block on a new blockchain successfully, called Bitcoin Cash at 18:24:41 UTC.

- Then, ViaBTC pool created a 1.9 MB BCH block that wasn't valid on the legacy Bitcoin network. This move, in fact, marked a break away from the major bitcoin network and taking the lead with a different technical plan.
- In general, the event occurred almost six hours after block 478,558 – the point at which miners made efforts to begin the split.
- Data from the network reveals that the BCH block had 6,985 transactions, with a block size of 1.915 MB which was almost two times the size of this parameter on the original chain. The data point is noteworthy since BCH was intended to boost network capacity by providing a blockchain with a bigger block size.

SUPPORT FROM BITCOIN PROVIDERS

As long as your Bitcoins are securely held in a personal wallet, the likelihood of losing your cashcoins is very slim. But, there is a slim chance that malicious miners could attempt to pilfer your coins when you attempt to make Bitcoin transactions. In trying to prevent this risk from occurring you may have to divide the coins into different Bitcoin and Bitcoin Cash wallets. Some wallets have given specific updates, services, and instructions for splitting coins.

Ahead of the August 1st, 2017 events, some major exchanges, and wallet providers gave their strategy for the hard fork. Many stated that they wouldn't back BCH at all; some said they would support it as an altcoin that will let users split their coins if they want.

But none of the businesses affirmed that they would back BCH as the number one, genuine Bitcoin. As an alternative, they declared an intention to support Bitcoin itself, or endorse the longest chain, which means that they would support any of the blockchain that emerged triumphantly.

Below are a list of leading Bitcoin exchanges and their position on sustaining BCH trading dated August 2017.

- Coinbase: will reject BCH
- BitMEX: will reject BCH
- Bitstamp: will reject BCH
- Bittrex: agreed
- Kraken: agreed
- OkCoin: agreed
- Poloniex: Possibly
- BTCC: agreed
- Gemini: will wait to see if BCH is viable
- Fitbit: will reject BCH
- ViaBTC: Yes, at a 1:1 ratio

Important note:

The most of above Bitcoin exchanges, which initially rejected Bitcoin cash trading, are altered their vision after lawsuits and pressure from the Bitcoin user community and decided the support the trade of Bitcoin cash in the (near) future.

From its website, wallets that support Bitcoin cash (BCH) ahead of the 1st of August event include the following:

- BitcoinUnlimited
- BitcoinABC
- Ledger
- ElectrumCash
- FreeWallet
- BitcoinClassic
- BXT
- Trezor
- BTC.com
- AirBitz
- Coinomi

Some major wallets have the following opinion about BCH:

Blockchain.info

It is crucial that owners of Blockchain wallets retain their wallet and associated recovery phrase and not delete them, even though they may empty the BTC balance. It supports withdrawals from exchanges that won't support BCH.

Electrum

Despite the fact that the most recent version of Electrum, 2.9, is able to make a distinction between rival chains, Electrum doesn't back Bitcoin Cash formally. In reality, Electrum believes the "Electrum Cash" fork of their software to be a trademark violation.

Ledger

Ledger is a trendy hardware wallet that supports Bitcoin Cash. Also, its wallet interface will feature a split utility and a selector for the two chains.

Exodus

Exodus doubles as a wallet and exchange service outlet, and doesn't provide support for BCH, either via splitting or providing a market.

Jaxx

Users on this platform are usually in charge of their private keys, and matching Bitcoin Cash (BCH) ought to be secure in your Jaxx wallet. But, users have to bear in mind that they won't be able to access/send/receive their Bitcoin Cash (BCH) pending when the integration occurs.

7: AFTERMATH OF THE BITCOIN SPLIT

BTC AND BCH

Some days after Bitcoin (BTC) had gone through an upgrade and a currency split, the foremost Cryptocurrency looks as if it has outlived one of the most tumultuous periods in its lifetime. The question you'd want to ask is, how has Bitcoin fared after this controversial and massive split? The outcome has thus far been splendid for Bitcoin. Everything appears to be getting back to normal, as confidence in the currency continues to soar with miners, traders, exchanges, and users of Bitcoin all going about their business as usual.

On the day that the split took place, the price of BTC which had been on a recovery to its former level a few days before August 1st, 2017, fell in value from \$2,875 to \$2718, representing about 5% drop. On the other hand, Bitcoin Cash (BCH) surpassed Ripple to turn out to be the third largest cryptocurrency, by trading at around \$400 levels. Some few hours later BCH's price movement became livelier and was trading in the region of \$700 and having a market capitalization that went past \$11 billion, representing nearly11% of the general market capitalization.

THE IMPACT OF THE SPLIT ON ETHERIUM

Some days before the split, Bitcoin (BTC) dropped about 10% to below $2,500 level in value owing to uncertainty over the impending upgrade and split. But it on the 1st of August, Ethereum (ETH) experienced a rise that pushed it tidily clear of $220 levels.

WHAT DOES THE FUTURE HOLD FOR BTC AND BCH

As at the time of writing this ebook, Bitcoin (BTC) just flew past the $3,500 level, which indicates a high degree of confidence in the number one cryptocurrency. With the second phase of the implementation of its upgrade still looming ahead on 1st of November 2017, which is a hard fork that is not backward compatible with older Bitcoin clients and will double the Bitcoin's block size to 2MB. When the result is coupled with the increase in block size limit that SEGWIT will bring about, then Bitcoin (BTC) should have a total maximum of 8MB of block space.

If the upgrade goes according to plan, then Bitcoin should continue to soar. Expectedly, BTC ought to continue with its rise in value than other cryptocurrencies and keep on enjoying a majority of the market capitalization. Perhaps we might see it reaching the $5,000 before the end of the year. It should remain safe and secure to use, but it would be hard to tell how its processing speed will be like in future. Furthermore, if other stakeholders in the community feel some of the core principles of Bitcoin such as its decentralized nature and democratic potentials of the blockchain technology is being compromised, then they might move on to other cryptocurrencies that have exciting possibilities and appeals to them.

As for BCH, it is currently trading (august 2017) at $340 but may likely rise in value in due time, if it is able to get miners to invest sufficient hash power to its network. Several estimates have it that BCH is able to attract 4% of miners to itself, making it vulnerable to attacks from malicious actors who manage some of these computing powers, and the only way they can prevent such attacks is to get close 50% of the Bitcoin's hash rate. That's why BCH's value might be just a fraction of BTC in the long run. However, if the SEGWIT changes make a lot of people unhappy, and they decide to switch over to BCH then its hash power might go up considerably.

Thank you!

Thank you again for buying this book!

I hope this book was able to help you to understand more regarding the technical language used in the world of Bitcoin and cryptocurrencies in general.

A gift as a thank you!

The cryptocurrency world is a fast moving world. Knowledge is power and the world of the cryptocurrencies keeps evolving.

If you want to stay up-to-date, please check out the author's website:

www.aboutcryptocurrencies.net.

Here you will find the latest cryptocurrencies news gathered from around the world and updated multiple times per day. Sign-up for the 'Daily Crypto News' and receive the electronic version of the officially published book: 'Bitcoin: What is Bitcoin?' for free as a thank you for buying this book.

So go to www.aboutcryptocurrencies.net, sign up and get the **ebook for free** as a thank you.

Finally, if you enjoyed this book, then I'd like to ask you for a favor, would you be kind enough to leave a review for this book on Amazon? It'd be greatly appreciated!

Go to below link to leave a review for this book on Amazon! https://www.amazon.com/dp/1986978737/

Thank you for reading and I want to wish you the best in the world of cryptocurrencies.

And you know, only make educated decisions!

Yours sincerely,

Johan von Amsterdam

Check out my other book about Bitcoin

Bitcoin: What is Bitcoin?

Unlock the Mystery of Bitcoin

No, it's not a trend. Yes, you need to get in the game. In this informative, must-have guide, you will discover all you need to know about Bitcoin, including how to set up your wallet, the best apps for mobile devices, and how to buy your first bitcoins.

We'll start from the beginning, learning about Bitcoin history and the numerous advantages Bitcoin investing has over government-controlled money. We will teach you how to protect your Bitcoin investments, introducing you to the block chain technology and the smart contracts principle.

After reading this book you will be able to:

- Build Your Own Web Wallet
- Know How to Buy Bitcoins
- Acquire Bitcoins for Free
- Decide Where to Keep Your Bitcoins

- Develop Strategies for Protecting Your Bitcoin Investments
- Understand Different Investment Strategies
- Talk Knowledgeably About Bitcoins

Crypto currencies are the future - don't miss out!

Get in the game now and buy this book today!

www.ingramcontent.com/pod-product-compliance
Lightning Source LLC
Chambersburg PA
CBHW030054230526
45471CB00003B/1086